Financial Ratios Analysis Guide

A Step by Step Guide to Balance Sheet and
Profit and Loss Statement Analysis

By Meir Liraz

(Including 10 Special Bonuses)

Published by Liraz Publishing

www.BizMove.com

Copyright © Liraz Publishing. All rights reserved.

ISBN: 9781695164741

Table of Contents

1. Introduction	5
2. Current Ratios	6
3. Quick Ratios	7
4. Working Capital	8
5. Leverage Ratio	9
6. Gross Margin Ratio	10
7. Net Profit Margin Ratio	11
8. Inventory Turnover Ratio	12
9. Accounts Receivable Turnover Ratio	13
10. Return on Assets Ratio	13
11. Return on Investment (ROI) Ratio	14
12. Understanding Financial Statements	15
13. Break Even Analysis Guide	23
14. Special Free Bonuses	36

MEIR LIRAZ

FINANCIAL RATIOS ANALYSIS GUIDE

1. Introduction

If you are not fully familiar with the structure of financial statements please read first chapter 12: Understanding Financial Statements.

What is ratio analysis? The Balance Sheet and the Statement of Income are essential, but they are only the starting point for successful financial management. Apply Ratio Analysis to Financial Statements to analyze the success, failure, and progress of your business.

Ratio Analysis enables the business owner/manager to spot trends in a business and to compare its performance and condition with the average performance of similar businesses in the same industry. To do this compare your ratios with the average of businesses similar to yours and compare your own ratios for several successive years, watching especially for any unfavorable trends that may be starting. Ratio analysis may provide the all-important early warning indications that allow you to solve your business problems before your business is destroyed by them.

Balance Sheet Ratio Analysis

Important Balance Sheet Ratios measure liquidity and solvency (a business's ability to pay its bills as they come due) and leverage (the extent to which the business is dependent on creditors' funding). They include the following ratios:

Liquidity Ratios

These ratios indicate the ease of turning assets into cash. They include the Current Ratio, Quick Ratio, and Working Capital.

2. Current Ratios

The Current Ratio is one of the best known measures of financial strength. It is figured as shown below:

Current Ratio =

$$\frac{\text{Total Current Assets}}{\text{Total Current Liabilities}}$$

The main question this ratio addresses is: "Does your business have enough current assets to meet the payment schedule of its current debts with a margin of safety for possible losses in current assets, such as inventory shrinkage or collectable accounts?" A generally acceptable current ratio is 2 to 1. But whether or not a specific ratio is satisfactory depends on the nature of the business and the characteristics of its current assets and liabilities. The minimum acceptable current ratio is obviously 1:1, but that relationship is usually playing it too close for comfort.

If you decide your business's current ratio is too low, you may be able to raise it by:

Paying some debts.

Increasing your current assets from loans or other borrowings with a maturity of more than one year.

Converting non-current assets into current assets.

Increasing your current assets from new equity contributions.

Putting profits back into the business.

3. Quick Ratios

The Quick Ratio is sometimes called the "acid-test" ratio and is one of the best measures of liquidity. It is figured as shown below:

$$\text{Quick Ratio} = \frac{\text{Cash} + \text{Government Securities} + \text{Receivables}}{\text{Total Current Liabilities}}$$

The Quick Ratio is a much more exacting measure than the Current Ratio. By excluding inventories, it concentrates on the really liquid assets, with value that is fairly certain. It helps answer the question: "If all sales revenues should disappear, could my business meet its current obligations with the readily convertible `quick' funds on hand?"

An acid-test of 1:1 is considered satisfactory unless the majority of your "quick assets" are in accounts receivable, and the pattern of accounts receivable collection lags behind the schedule for paying current liabilities.

4. Working Capital

Working Capital is more a measure of cash flow than a ratio. The result of this calculation must be a positive number. It is calculated as shown below:

Working Capital = Total Current Assets - Total Current Liabilities

Bankers look at Net Working Capital over time to determine a company's ability to weather financial crises. Loans are often tied to minimum working capital requirements.

A general observation about these three Liquidity Ratios is that the higher they are the better, especially if you are relying to any significant extent on creditor money to finance assets.

5. Leverage Ratio

This Debt/Worth or Leverage Ratio indicates the extent to which the business is reliant on debt financing (creditor money versus owner's equity):

Debt/Worth Ratio =

$$\frac{\text{Total Liabilities}}{\text{Net Worth}}$$

Generally, the higher this ratio, the more risky a creditor will perceive its exposure in your business, making it correspondingly harder to obtain credit.

Income Statement Ratio Analysis

The following important State of Income Ratios measure profitability:

6. Gross Margin Ratio

This ratio is the percentage of sales dollars left after subtracting the cost of goods sold from net sales. It measures the percentage of sales dollars remaining (after obtaining or manufacturing the goods sold) available to pay the overhead expenses of the company.

Comparison of your business ratios to those of similar businesses will reveal the relative strengths or weaknesses in your business. The Gross Margin Ratio is calculated as follows:

Gross Margin Ratio =

$$\frac{\text{Gross Profit}}{\text{Net Sales}}$$

(Gross Profit = Net Sales - Cost of Goods Sold)

7. Net Profit Margin Ratio

This ratio is the percentage of sales dollars left after subtracting the Cost of Goods sold and all expenses, except income taxes. It provides a good opportunity to compare your company's "return on sales" with the performance of other companies in your industry. It is calculated before income tax because tax rates and tax liabilities vary from company to company for a wide variety of reasons, making comparisons after taxes much more difficult. The Net Profit Margin Ratio is calculated as follows:

Net Profit Margin Ratio =

$$\frac{\text{Net Profit Before Tax}}{\text{Net Sales}}$$

Management Ratios

Other important ratios, often referred to as Management Ratios, are also derived from Balance Sheet and Statement of Income information.

8. Inventory Turnover Ratio

This ratio reveals how well inventory is being managed. It is important because the more times inventory can be turned in a given operating cycle, the greater the profit. The Inventory Turnover Ratio is calculated as follows:

Inventory Turnover Ratio =

$$\frac{\text{Net Sales}}{\text{Average Inventory at Cost}}$$

9. Accounts Receivable Turnover Ratio

This ratio indicates how well accounts receivable are being collected. If receivables are not collected reasonably in accordance with their terms, management should rethink its collection policy. If receivables are excessively slow in being converted to cash, liquidity could be severely impaired. The Accounts Receivable Turnover Ratio is calculated as follows:

$$\frac{\text{Net Credit Sales/Year}}{\text{365 Days/Year}} = \text{Daily Credit Sales}$$

$$\text{Accounts Receivable Turnover (in days)} = \frac{\text{Accounts Receivable}}{\text{Daily Credit Sales}}$$

10. Return on Assets Ratio

This measures how efficiently profits are being generated from the assets employed in the business when compared with the ratios of firms in a similar business. A low ratio in comparison with industry averages indicates an inefficient use of business assets. The Return on Assets Ratio is calculated as follows:

Return on Assets =

$$\frac{\text{Net Profit Before Tax}}{\text{Total Assets}}$$

11. Return on Investment (ROI) Ratio.

The ROI is perhaps the most important ratio of all. It is the percentage of return on funds invested in the business by its owners. In short, this ratio tells the owner whether or not all the effort put into the business has been worthwhile. If the ROI is less than the rate of return on an alternative, risk-free investment such as a bank savings account, the owner may be wiser to sell the company, put the money in such a savings instrument, and avoid the daily struggles of small business management. The ROI is calculated as follows:

$$\text{Return on Investment} = \frac{\text{Net Profit before Tax}}{\text{Net Worth}}$$

These Liquidity, Leverage, Profitability, and Management Ratios allow the business owner to identify trends in a business and to compare its progress with the performance of others through data published by various sources. The owner may thus determine the business's relative strengths and weaknesses.

12. Understanding Financial Statements

Financial Statements analysis record the performance of your business and allow you to diagnose its strengths and weaknesses by providing a written summary of financial activities. There are two primary financial statements: the Balance Sheet and the Statement of Income.

The Balance Sheet

Financial statement analysis looks first at the balance sheet. The Balance Sheet provides a picture of the financial health of a business at a given moment, usually at the close of an accounting period. It lists in detail those material and intangible items the business owns (known as its assets) and what money the business owes, either to its creditors (liabilities) or to its owners (shareholders' equity or net worth of the business).

Assets include not only cash, merchandise inventory, land, buildings, equipment, machinery, furniture, patents, trademarks, and the like, but also money due from individuals or other businesses (known as accounts or notes receivable).

Liabilities are funds acquired for a business through loans or the sale of property or services to the business on credit. Creditors do not acquire business ownership, but promissory notes to be paid at a designated future date.

Shareholders' equity (or net worth or capital) is money put into a business by its owners for use by the business in acquiring assets.

At any given time, a business's assets equal the total contributions by the creditors and owners, as illustrated by the following formula for the Balance Sheet:

Assets = Liabilities + Net worth

This formula is a basic premise of accounting. If a business owes more money to creditors than it possesses in value of assets owned, the net worth or owner's equity of the business will be a negative number.

The Balance Sheet is designed to show how the assets, liabilities, and net worth of a business are distributed at any given time. It is usually prepared at regular intervals; e.g., at each month's end, but especially at the end of each fiscal (accounting) year.

By regularly preparing this summary of what the business owns and owes (the Balance Sheet), the business owner/manager can identify and analyze trends in the financial strength of the business. It permits timely modifications, such as gradually decreasing the amount of money the business owes to creditors and increasing the amount the business owes its owners.

All Balance Sheets contain the same categories of assets, liabilities, and net worth. Assets are arranged in decreasing order of how quickly they can be turned into cash (liquidity). Liabilities are listed in order of how soon they must be repaid, followed by retained earnings (net worth or owner's equity).

The categories and format of the Balance Sheet are established by a system known as Generally Accepted Accounting Principles (GAAP). The system is applied to all companies, large or small, so anyone reading the Balance Sheet can readily understand the story it tells.

Balance Sheet - ABC Company
December 31, XXX1

Cash	18,960
Accounts Receivable	14,560
Inventory	68,220
Total Current Assets	101,740
Equipment and Fixtures	11,680
Prepaid Expenses	12,780
Total Assets	126,200
Notes Payable, Bank	20,000
Accounts Payable	22,400
Accruals	9,400
Total Current Liabilities	51,800
Total Liabilities	51,800
Net Worth*	74,400
Total Liabilities and Net Worth	126,200

*Assets - Liabilities = New Worth

Balance Sheet Categories

Assets and liabilities are broken down into categories as described as follows:.

Assets: An asset is anything the business owns that has monetary value.

Current Assets include cash, government securities, marketable securities, accounts receivable, notes receivable (other than from officers or employees), inventories, prepaid expenses, and any other item that could be converted into cash within one year in the normal course of business.

Fixed Assets are those acquired for long-term use in a business such as land, plant, equipment, machinery, leasehold improvements, furniture, fixtures, and any other items with an expected useful business life measured in years (as opposed to items that will wear out or be used up in less than one year and are usually expensed when they are purchased). These assets are typically not for resale and are recorded in the Balance Sheet at their net cost less accumulated depreciation.

Other Assets include intangible assets, such as patents, royalty arrangements, copyrights, exclusive use contracts, and notes receivable from officers and employees.

Liabilities: Liabilities are the claims of creditors against the assets of the business (debts owed by the business).

Current Liabilities are accounts payable, notes payable to banks, accrued expenses (wages, salaries), taxes payable, the current portion (due within one year) of long-term debt, and other obligations to creditors due within one year.

Long-Term Liabilities are mortgages, intermediate and long-term bank loans, equipment loans, and any other obligation for money due to a creditor with a maturity longer than one year.

Net Worth is the assets of the business minus its liabilities. Net worth equals the owner's equity. This equity is the investment by the owner plus any profits or minus any losses that have accumulated in the business.

The Statement of Income

The second primary report included in a business's Financial Statement is the Statement of Income. The Statement of Income is a measurement of a company's sales and expenses over a specific period of time. It is also prepared at regular intervals (again, each month and fiscal year end) to show the results of operating during those accounting periods. It too follows Generally Accepted

Accounting Principles (GAAP) and contains specific revenue and expense categories regardless of the nature of the business.

Statement of Income Categories

The Statement of Income categories are calculated as described below:

Net Sales (gross sales less returns and allowances)

Less Cost of Goods Sold (cost of inventories)

Equals Gross Margin (gross profit on sales before operating expenses)

Less Selling and Administrative Expenses (salaries, wages, payroll taxes and benefits, rent, utilities, maintenance expenses, office supplies, postage, automobile/vehicle expenses, insurance, legal and accounting expenses, depreciation)

Equals Operating Profit (profit before other non-operating income or expense)

Plus Other Income (income from discounts, investments, customer charge accounts)

Less Other Expenses (interest expense)

Equals Net Profit (or Loss) before Tax (the figure on which your tax is calculated)

Less Income Taxes (if any are due)

Equals Net Profit (or Loss) After Tax

Income Statement - ABC Company
December 31,XXX1

Net Sales		681,160
Cost of Goods Sold		476,960
Gross Profit on Sales		204,200
Expenses:		
Wages	69,480	
Delivery Expenses	9,540	
Bad Debts Allowances	4,090	
Communications	2,040	
Depreciation Allowance	4,090	
Insurance	6,130	
Taxes	10,210	
Advertising	15,660	
Interest	4,090	
Other Charges	7,490	
Total Expenses		132,820
Net Profit		71,380
Other Income		8,860
Total Net Income		80,240

Calculating the Cost of Goods Sold

Calculation of the Cost of Goods Sold category in the Statement of Income (or Profit-and-Loss Statement as it is sometimes called) varies depending on whether the business is retail, wholesale, or manufacturing. In retailing and wholesaling, computing the cost of goods sold during the accounting period involves beginning and ending inventories. This, of course, includes purchases made during the accounting period. In manufacturing it involves not only finished-goods inventories, but also raw materials inventories, goods-in-process inventories, direct labor, and direct factory overhead costs.

Regardless of the calculation for Cost of Goods Sold, deduct the Cost of Goods Sold from Net Sales to get Gross Margin or Gross Profit. From Gross Profit, deduct general or indirect overhead, such as selling expenses, office expenses, and interest expenses. To calculate your Net Profit. This is the final profit after all costs and expenses for the accounting period have been deducted.

13. Break Even Analysis Guide

Break-even analysis is not a panacea. It doesn't tell you if your costs are out of line. It tells you only what sales volume you need to cover fixed costs.

It is, however, an excellent starting point for finding out where you are and, more importantly, where you can go. It's a good first step to planning.

This chapter presented as a conversation between a business counselor (C) and the owner-manager of a retail store (M), discusses a simplified method of calculating the break-even point for a retail operation. While this method is not appropriate for manufacturers, it does provide a financial planning take-off point.

M: I'm ready to expand. I've just had a great forth quarter. I've got a chance to move to a larger store in a good location. I really think I'm on my way. Still, though, I don't want to take any unnecessary chances and lose what I've built up these first three years. What do you think I should do?

C: Let me answer your question with a question: What's your break-even point now and what will it be if you assume the added expansion cost?

M: I'm not exactly sure, but after that last quarter, I've got money in the bank and I'm paying all my bills on time.

What Bank Balances May Not Reveal

C: I'm glad to hear you're in good shape, but you can't make an intelligent expansion decision based on your bank balance at a given moment.

M: You ought to know, but why not

C: Take your balance now, for example. It's a lot better than it was at the end of the first quarter, isn't it?

M: Sure, but the first quarter's usually slow. It's a fact of retail life.

C: And the fourth quarter is usually good, right?

M: Yes, that a fact, too. But mine was outstanding - it was the best I've ever had.

C: I'm sure it was, but it can distort the picture. If you're relying on your bank balance for a feel for your break-even point, you may just be guessing. Many things influence your bank balance that may not necessarily have a direct bearing on the break-even point for your store. Seasonal fluctuation is just one of them.

M: There are more?

C: Sure, capital expenditures, extraordinary repairs, unusual outlay...

M: Okay, I get the point. My bank balance is meaningless. I shouldn't expand.

C: We don't know that yet. After we find out what sales volume you'll need to break even, then you'll tell me if you ought to expand or not.

M: Some counselor. First you tell me I don't know what I'm doing and then you expect me to advise me on expansion.

Break-even Analysis Is Not a Substitute for Judgment

C: You're wrong on the first half of that; I know you know retailing. But, yes, you'll decide on the basis of your business knowledge and judgment whether or not expansion now makes sense.

M: I must do something right. I'm still in business.

C: Exactly. You've made it through some of the toughest business years, the first ones. And you're showing a fair profit. I think you've got a real flair for merchandising.

M: Please, you'll make me blush. What about this break-even thing?

What Break-Even Means

C: Break-even is simply the point where costs equal what you're taking in - no profit, no loss - over a relevant sales range. To calculate this point you must work with only two factors, fixed expenses (like insurance or rent) and variable costs (like cost of goods or sales commissions).

M: I sure wish my costs were fixed. Everything goes up for me. My insurance, for example, looks like it's going up 25 percent over last year.

Fixed and Variable Costs

C: Well, actually "fixed costs" is something of a misnomer. Sure, rents, property taxes, insurance, even the salary you pay yourself may fluctuate - but on a yearly basis and not in relation to sales. For the purpose of break-even analysis every cost that doesn't vary in relation to sales is called "fixed". Your rent, for instance, stays the same for a year whether you sell 250,000 or 2.50 worth of goods, though we know some rents are tied to volume and vary. The same is usually true of utilities, depreciation and similar expense items.

M: I see the point. Variable costs, then, are basically my cost of sales? I have to buy more if I sell more. If I paid commissions, I'd be paying more for more sales, and that sort of thing.

C: That's right. There can be other variable costs, but we're simplifying. In addition, you'll probably find costs that seem to be part variable, part fixed.

M: You mean they're "semi-variable" or "semi-fixed?"

C: Yes, they're costs that remain fixed up to a certain sales volume and then jump as that volume is exceeded. For example, office costs, or delivery expenses may fit in this category.

M: How do I treat them?

C: Use your good business judgment and split them between fixed and variable costs in what you consider a reasonable proportion. The important thing is to hold in mind for simple break-even analysis is to keep it simple. Over simplicity is, of course, a drawback of this method. But simple break-even analysis really helps you to see your way into a planning problem and to establish its perimeters.

M: I like the idea of simplicity, but I don't think break-even sounds simple so far.

C: I think you'll see how easy it is if we work through an example. Here, take a look at this hypothetical income or profit and loss statement for the B-E Retail Store.

B-E Retail Store - Income Statement

Item		Amount	Percent
Sales		60,000	100
Cost of Sales		42,000	70
Gross Profit		18,000	30
Expenses:			
Rent	1,800		3
Wages	12,600		21
Utilities	2,400		4
Insurance	1,200		2
Taxes	600		1
All Other	600		1
Total Expenses		19,200	32
Loss for period		(1,200)	(2)

FINANCIAL RATIOS ANALYSIS GUIDE

M: B-E doesn't seem to have broken even.

C: Correct. Let's find out what kind of sales volume B-E needed to break-even in that year. For simplicity (there's that word again) Let's consider cost of sales (which is 70 percent of sales) as the total variable costs and the expense items of 19,200 as the fixed costs. We calculate the break-even point by using an algebraic formula.

M: A simple one, I hope.

C: Of course. It's just $S = F + V$, where:

S = Sales at the break-even point,

F = Fixed expenses, and

V = Variable costs and expenses as a percent of sales.

M: All right, we know B-E's variable and fixed costs. How do we get sales?

C: Let's plug in the figures:

$S = 19,200 + .70S$

$10S = 192,000 + 7S$

O-M: Excuse me, 10S?

C: I multiplied the whole equation by 10 to get rid

of the decimal fraction, because I think it's easier to work with whole numbers.

Anyway, we get:

10S - 7S = 192,00

3S = 192,000

S = 64,000

M: B-E needed 64,000 total sales to break even? Anything less, they'd have a loss; anything more they'd make a profit?

C: You've got it. Let's check it, though, just to confirm it:

Sales	64,000	
Less Cost of Sales	-44,800	(70% of sales)
Gross Profit	19,200	
Less Expenses	-19,200	
Profit or Loss	0	

M: Okay, so B-E has broken even. I think they'd like to make a profit. I know I do.

Calculating Break-even for a Given Profit

C: We can find out what kind of sales B-E needed to make a profit using the formula again. Leaving the other figures the same, let's put in a modest profit - say, 9,000 - and see what sales they needed. The formula now looks like this:

Sales = Fixed Expenses + Variable Costs + Profit.

M: You just add the desired amount of profit in?

C: Yes, really it affects the break-even point just like a fixed expense:

$S = 19{,}200 + .70S + 9{,}000$ (desired profit)

$10S = 192{,}000 + 7S + 90{,}000$ (multiple by 10 to eliminate fraction)

$3S = 282{,}000$

$S = 94{,}000$

M: May I check the figures this time?

C: Certainly.

M: All right, let's see:

Sales	94,000
Less Cost of Sales	-65,800 (70% of sales)
Gross Profit	28,200
Less Expenses	-19,000
Profit	9,000

C: Convinced?

M: Yes, I can see how this formula can help you find how much you need to sell to break even or make a given profit, but what about my problem?

Break-even Analysis for Planning

C: Break-even analysis is just what you need. It's primarily a planning tool. I've looked at your Income Statement and divided it into fixed and variable costs. As I see it, your cost of sales, which we'll consider as your total variable costs, comes to about 60 percent of sales. Your fixed expenses ran about 60,000. So for last year:

$S = 60,000 + .60S$

$10S = 600,000 + 6S$

$4S = 600,000$

$S = 150,000$

You had to sell only 150,000 worth of merchandise to break even.

M: As you can see, I sold 200,000 worth, but I didn't make a 50,000 profit.

C: Right, you made a 20,000 profit just as the bottom line indicates. Remember, you still had those variable costs on sales even after all of your fixed expenses were covered at the 150,000 level.

M: Oh, I see, it's like this:

$S = F + V + \text{Profit}$

$S = 60,000 + .60S = 20,000$

$10S = 600,000 + 6S + 200,000$

$4S = 800,000$

$S = 200,000$

C: Now you've got it. Let's consider your expansion question. How much will your rent increase?

Using Break-even Analysis to Examine Expansion Feasibility

M: It would be about 5,000 more. I figure the utilities for the larger space will be 2,000 more than I paid last year. Taxes, the "fixed" ones, I expect to run about 500, I also think I may need to hire another sales person.

C: Let's say you do. What do you plan to pay?

M: I'd pay an experienced sales clerk about 9,000. I'm toying with the idea of instituting a 2 percent commission on sales as an incentive, too.

C: All right. We know it's not as simple as we'll lay it out, but I think the analysis will give you an idea of whether or not to explore the expansion idea more carefully and in greater detail.

M: Fine

C: Your fixed expenses will rise by 17,500, if you include hiring another employee. That brings them to 77,500, assuming no other increases from last year's 60,000. For simplicity's sake let's assume your cost of sales (your variable costs) will increase only by the 2 percent commission. That means 62 percent of sales for variable costs. so:

$S = 77,500 + .62S$

$100S = 7,774,000 + 62S$ (multiplied by 100 to eliminate fraction)

$38S = 7,775,000$

$S = 205,000$ (approximately)

M: Only 5,000 more than I did last year? I can do that easily.

C: And be 20,000 in profits worse off than last year. Let's put last year's 20,000 profit in - in an expansion you still might want to do at least as well:

$S = 77,500 + .62S + 22,000$

$100S = 7,750,000 + 62S + 2,000,000$

$38S = 9,750,000$

$S = 257,000$ (approximately)

M: Hm, that's approximately a 25 percent sales increase just to make the same profit as last year.

Business Judgment Still Necessary

C: Do you think you can boost sales by that much? Perhaps you see long range benefits from expansion that justify sacrificing some profit for the short run.

M: I'm not sure. I'll have to give it more thought, look at the trends in my business and in this area. My pricing policy may need adjustment. Maybe I can cut costs. But now at least I've got a starting point, a dollar figure I can work with and from. Most importantly of all, I have a technique to help me attack my problem and help point me toward a rational decision.

C: That's what break-even analysis is all about.

14. Special Free Bonuses

You can access your free bonuses here:

https://www.bizmove.com/bizgifts.htm

Here's what you get:

#1 How to Be a Good Manager and Leader; 120 Tips to improve your Leadership Skills (Leadership Video Guide).

Learn how to improve your leadership skills and become a better manager and leader. Here's how to be the boss people want to give 200 percent for. In this video you'll discover 120 powerful tips and strategies to motivate and inspire your people to bring out the best in them.

#2 Small Business Management: Essential Ingredients for Success (eBook Guide)

Discover scores of business management tricks, secrets and shortcuts. This Ebook guide does far more than impart knowledge - it inspires action.

#3 How to Manage Yourself for Success; 90 Tips to Better Manage Yourself and Your Time (Self Management Video Guide)

You are responsible for everything that happens in your life. Learn to accept total responsibility for yourself. If you don't manage yourself, then you are letting others have control of your life. In this video you'll discover 90 powerful tips and strategies to better manage yourself for success.

#4 80 Best Inspirational Quotes for Success (Motivational Video Guide)

For this video we scanned thousands of motivational and inspirational quotes to bring you this collection of the best 80 motivational quotes for success in life.

#5 Top 10 Habits to Adopt From Highly Successful People (Self Growth Video Guide)

In this video you'll discover the top 10 habits of

highly successful people that you can adopt and achieve success in your life.

#6 Personal Branding: How to Make a Killer First Impression (Self Promotion Video Guide)

This video deals with personal branding. While promoting your personal brand, you'll discover in this video the ten most effective things you can do to make the best first impression possible.

#7 How to Advance Your Career 10 Times Faster (Career Advancement Video Guide)

The most important thing to remember about your career today is that you need to be responsible for your own future. In this video you'll discover 10 powerful strategies to advance your career faster.

#8 How to Get Success in Life; 10 Strategies to Attract the Life You Want (Self Actualization Video Guide)

To have more, we must be more of who we are. The secret is in the doing; none of it matters until we do something about it. In this video you'll discover 10 powerful strategies to attract the life you want.

#9 A Comprehensive Package of Business Tools

Here's a collection featuring dozens of business related templates, worksheets, forms, and plans; covering finance, starting a business, marketing, business planning, sales, and general management.

#10 People Management Skills: How to Deal with Difficult Employees (Managing People Video Guide)

Problem behavior on the part of employees can erupt for a variety of reasons. In this video you'll discover the top ten ideas for dealing with difficult employees.

* * * *

www.ingramcontent.com/pod-product-compliance
Lightning Source LLC
Chambersburg PA
CBHW070843220526
45466CB00002B/867